is now friends with
BABYBOOMER.

Social Media's Twitter and Facebook That's So True's,
Do's & Dont's

You'll laugh
You'll cry
You'll want to *send* the Babyboomers back to Woodstock
World War II offspring will want to *report* you
You'll *ignore* your High-School Teacher's *friend request*

BEN POPP

The Digitally-Dug Ground Worm
For The Hungrier Social Media Hatchling

Any and all stress, annoyances, bugaboos, built up "LOL" hatred you received from social media platforms,I promise you, will be removed from your blogging soul once you've reached book's end. The truth-revealing and perhaps arguable text once deemed-nonsensical, you'll find in these passages are grand enough factors in scale, to make or break the existing or future fate of social media startups as well as answer the begging question of: Is this "click-happy, stay indoors lifestyle", breeding an introverted nation?

Youth Majority Approved: Yes... Babyboomer Approved: Pending... Original Woodstock Patrons Approved: Pending...
Hoodrat Approved: Pending... Entrepreneurs Launching Social Media Approved: Pending...
Parent Approved: Pending...

To all of you LEGITIMATE social media platform users.

Reader: "I caught some misspelled words & grammatical errors!"

Author: Purposely orchestrated to depict current social media..

Warning: Book is for those who can HANDLE Humor

#sillyboomer,socialmedias4kids

2013 copyright.

Preface

It says on the cover that I, Ben Popp wrote this. But, that couldn't be farther from the truth.. Truth is, I wasn't supposed to be talking about my findings to ANYBODY; especially publicly.. This book you've chosen to read here, is actually derived from the diary of a recently deceased social media addict. I used to do yard work for him, but he never came out of his dilapidated house. When he'd pay me my weekly wages, he stuck his hand through this custom box-like contraption he built on his door. I couldn't help but feeling like the #Lorax receiving a #Truffula seed from the #Wuncler.. Anyways, after a year of working for this digital hermit, he finally spoke to me. He never let me in his house, so I would stand there at his door on payday; and he would reveal to me possibly the most groundbreaking mysteries of life to ever to be exposed to the world:

"The Anatomy of Social Media Everything. A Fatal Dissection."

Each week it was like hearing about the first time Americans landed on the moon! His findings ever so colossal in scope, they were. My staying of an extra ten minutes or so at his mysterious door lasted for about a half a year. One Friday came and as usual I waited at the door. But, no one appeared. I waited there ten minutes before I built up enough courage to knock on that old Victorian door. The quivering hand never breached that contraption...Perhaps he's out of town? My thoughts rambled.. I stuck my grass-clipping covered hand through that contraption thinking that maybe he left my wages for me to grab. What I pulled out was a diary. A diary with such a vast amount of dust that I had to #Pledge it twice over.. As I peered down to that now lemon-scented diary, it hit me. My digitally distraught mentor had left me his life's work..

What now? I thought to myself.. I couldn't possibly be the only one to keep these societal breakthroughs to myself! How selfish of me that would be.. I was under no legal contract like Lawyer/Client Confidentiality with the man who possessed "the thousand-yard social platform stare." If I could leave humanity any gift, these passages from his diary, tops the list.

Rest In Peace Wi-Fi Wuncler.
1990-2013

#BOOMER SIGHTING!

Why are you *signed in*? Why are you *typing*?
Why are your political thoughts always griping?
Why do you start conversations in your niece's
profile pic *comment* box? Leaving *comments* like
"NICE PICTURE" or "LOOK AT THAT FOX"

-The Babyboomer..

Help me someone, I can't figure this out. My parents and relatives seem to never *LOG-OUT*! It's not like we talk about the old days at Woodstock.. At least would you turn off your dam CAPSLOCK!

–The Babyboomer..

"YOU'RE TROUBLE", "BETH HOW'S THE
KIDS?", "WHAT'S THIS HOOPLA ABOUT

THESE YOUTUBE VIDS?". "BACK IN MY DAY, THAT STUFF WOULD NEVER FLY!", "MY SON JUST *SIGNED ON*, I THINK I SHALL ONLY *TYPE* "HI"..

-The Babyboomer

Dale, did you speak to Christopher today? "Yeah for a bit, in business class today he learned to audit." I tried to call him but he didn't respond, you know what, I bet its his gal pal, that blonde! If he can't have the decency to answer his phone, read my texts, or sense my frantic tone. How come it says here on *Facebook* at half past nine, that he is "fuckin lit" and *online*?..

-Parent joining *Facebook*..

Kevin Kofax *liked* Democrats United. 2 minutes ago via android.

Kevin Kofax *liked* Non-Republican Party. 5 seconds ago after liking Democrats United.

Kevin Kofax *shared* Anti-Republican Best Newspaper Cartoons's.org's photo. 30 seconds ago

Kevin Kofax *logged-in* 5 hours later, then *liked* meme picture George Bush Takes Pie In Face. 10 seconds later

Kevin Kofax's *Friends* Suggested Kevin List "He Is Unaware His *Friends* Haven't Cared Nor Will Ever Care About His Public Political *Views, Posts, Shares* Since His *Account's* Inception Date."

-*Sent* His Now Former And Invisible *Friends* since Kevin's Misguided Decision To *Join*..

Who's Meagan? She *shared* your band's page. Is she the one who dated your singer Ian Cage?

Why didn't you respond to your grandmother's post? At that wedding gig you just played, how was the toast? Jeez your pal Steve, is that all he does is drink? Take pics with booze? What must his parents think? What does it mean when it says someone *wants to be your friend*? How can I make something on my *page trend* ?

-Un-pause The TV, Dad Trolls On..

It's one thing to see your ex with his next. It's one thing to *vine* your incoherent chum's text. It's one thing to *re-post* what your neighbor just ate. But it's NOT cool

to see what's clogging your *newsfeed* : Mom was
asked to *join* "Class of 78."

-Generation Glory Days..

Though *social media's* a hoot, most of the time, with its witty remarks, and dope rhymes. Not all things you *view*, will steady your hairs, like Baby Boomer banter on whose better "Packers" or "Bears." Mom *posting* never-ending maternal *memes*. Dad's one-word responses to co-worker *suggested* luau themes. Your high-school teacher adding you as a *friend*, this designated demographic will be a puzzle to the end.

–Coordinates of the Generational Gap? via
Everywhere You Look Online..

There once was a lady, who lived in a shoe. This lady had nothing but *tweeting* to do. She *tweeted* by day, *posted* by nights end. Realizing that it was herself..that SHE, should *de-friend*..

–An Individual Stares Into The LOL-Ridden
Abyss…

A *like* is a *like*, no matter the reason, no matter how forced, no matter which season.
A *like* will boost your *social status*, feeding the articulate inner web apparatus.

-If Only World Hunger Was Digital: *Posts, Events, Favorites* etc Would Provide Adequate Sustenance..

Some demand *tweets*, some demand *shares*, some reprimand those digital dares. Some demand cocktails after a long day's work, while some craft *events* that drive *friends* berserk...

-User Behavior Saviors...

If you stare into the abyss of your *profile inbox*, amongst your booty calls, amongst investment ads for gold at Fort Knox. Your stomach will twist,

your thoughts will dread. Seeing your Aunt's
message rehashing the holidays, STILL *unread*.

-Peering Into The Wonderball Of Platform
Gravity..

Looky what's this? A new *friend request* ? Of
what looks to be a super hot chick in a dress?
Checked out her *page*, saw not one *status*
release, you wont fool me, un-sneaky police.

-Law Enforcement Cyber Fishing Trips..

Really one *profile pic* ? Really no *About* ? Really no *hometown* or a *favorite* band like "No Doubt"? A supermodel *pic* ? Over one thousand *friends* ? Guess I could go out with this girl if I HAD #SEINFELD STIPENDS!

-Public Private Eye..

Hell Yeah i'm covered! She'll believe anything! Even when I told her about the tickets to #STING! I'm glad i'm here, eating this steak, its way better than your Grandma's wake. "Son smile big for the camera here!" Laughing from my gullet down to my rear. "Wow son your *picture* already got two *likes* !" Right then I new I was busted, yikes. I really thought my genius ought be listed in a dictionary or encyclopedia, but now I'm dumped thanks to Dad on *social media*...

-"Hey Son, Give Me A Hand Making My *Facebook* ?" Regrets…

I could just hide! I could just scream! When Mom says in public she's "got coupons to redeem!" As bad is "Honey you gotta see Aunt Cathy's *Re-Pin* ! Nothing's worse at the Post Office, when mom *Checks In...*

-Time To Hold Up Mom's Framed Pic Of Her
Backstage With *Friends* At A #RATT Concert..

Wait till I see him, I'll give him a piece of my mind. We'll see his response to "on the *event* my name was left be-hind!" Am I really that bad? Am I really that lame? Perhaps it's my digital upbringing that's to blame..

-Screwed Generation X…

When you hear the term "Be, the difference", it means *click* like your finger's a dancer. On the pressuring *meme pics* that all of your Mo-town *friends liked, like* "Drugs Are Bad, or Hate Cancer"..

–Babyboomer *Social Media* Etiquette Uncertainty..

This Christmas, I promise I will *share* my annual goals for the New Year publicly; in which none I shall keep.

This Christmas, I promise to *post* family party *pictures* almost IMMEDIATELY after they are taken, to my nearest *social media* platform.

This Christmas, I hope Santa rewards my actions of creating a *public figure page* on him and getting him *likes*.

–Recently Divorced, Dating Mother of Several Children..

Once in a land, quite far from town, dwelled a lad with a *pad*, sporting a *thumbs-down* causing frown. Could it be, that this lad from afar, was left afloat on a cyber-boat?

-Tomb Of The Unknown *Uploader*...

Aargh matees, bellowed the head *follower*. Quit yer bellyaching ya *un-invited* wallower. Gander

your eyes, not at the number of my crew. But
feast them upon my devoted adieu!

–Lost Journal Of The First Paparazzi
Swashbuckler..

It was ssssooo ssoo great seeing my family this weekend! I'll definitely keep you all *posted* when I have the official dates when Greg, I and the kids can come down for the weekend. For now I have the 5-8th of next month. It all depends on Greg's work schedule though. Oh, and my lovely niece: Are you ready for mojito night round 2! WOOT

WOOT! And sis, I 'll bring my hairdresser Trisha's brownie recipe I was raving about. Let's just hope this time when we bake that adorable Baxter doesn't get into the batter before we do! LOL!

–*Read* Everyone You Know, Against Their Will. This Everyone, Wants Those Two Minutes Of Their Lives Back..

Could a man named Pappy, really be happy, with the outcome of his selected *profile pic*? In a booth at the Moose, shirt drenched with hops juice, tonguing a VFW chick looking like Rocky Balboa's Trainer Mick?

–Making The Coherent Decision To *Post* A *Picture* Of Yourself Twenty Years Ago..

Checking-in here, *checking-in* there, *checking-in* at the deli, even the state fair. Remember to check the amount of times *checking- in*, leaving your digital doormat saying "Burglars, come in!"

-Your *Inbox* Is Full, Your Residence Is Not..

"Honey at work, there's my cute teaching aid, She's oh so sweet and danced in the parade! I told her about you and to look at my *page,* so she can catch a glimpse before curiosity fades." Oh no I thought! What have you done! That day I was hungover and hair wasn't done! Maybe she'll *search* me directly for fun, reality is she'll find Mom's forced family day one..

–The Relationship Hindering Guardian..

This classmate of mine, could he really be smart? Could he really be genius and sketch a periodic table chart? Could his lineage date back to early inventors? Could he in the future locate disease preventers? Could this undetected brainiac classmate of mine, possess other worldly premonition? Why else would he substitute his middle name on his *profile*, to Deondre "High Definition"?

-Hooked On Phonics Alumni..

Dang gurl use ffiinnee, My numba is three three fo. I swear imma keep possen *comments* even dough you neva *respond* befo. I finna no dat you be mines one day, I'd even bet all my cents. We could be like da tale of da urban Romeo an jewleeit, tanks to my charmin pisha comments.

-Department Of Corrections First Round Draft Picks..

Feed me.. Feed me not. Sustain thyself, with a *comment* or dot. Feed not my bodily gullet, but rather a taste of neighbors mullet. Just a peep of that new trailer or mouth-watering sound bite, to satisfy the hunger of my *social media* appetite.

-Your Closet *News-Feed* Refresher...

Riddle me this: I am always in front, first in line, never last, and a few keys from nine. Seen by *users* both domestic and foreign, used in any weather from heat waves to pourin. I'm on the faces of injured cartoons, to proceed I'm ordered to engage by automated buffoons. My use is only to make official, I am defective if put in front of an initial. I am?

-The #*Hashtag*…

Because of my actions, because of my flaws, you ripped out my soul, with your #KewpieDoll claws. My humor may be off color, my dissenting opinions may vary, but I know in my heart your *groups*, grow ever so weary.

–De-friending Karma Conspiracy…

Oh my quill. My dearest quill. Not a day goes by I
don't reminisce about your effective nature.
Should I get the chance to hold you again.. To
dip you in ink, and pen what I think..Oh to hold

you again my feathery fellow. What a difference it made to receive letter with "Hello." No more..No more my whale blubber injected fellow.

-Colonial Chap Meets Internet…

May the spirit of the digital world show *promotional* favor. May the wings of the *cropped* courier bring *page rank* with flavor. May the majestic movements of the wire-walker code X , *display* your everything to this world ,the *following* and the *next*.

-Philosophically *Signed-In*..

In the past I never really had that something, or special someone to live for. That special someone who since freshman year I could adore. Baby you are my rock when tough times hit. If I could reach through this screen I'd kiss you a bit. You make me laugh, I felt comfortable around you to cry. The flame we share will never die. Happy three months baby.

–For Crushes That Cringe, Insecurity Shall Binge..

Today I realized what it means to really care for someone. It means to be there for them through the good and the bad. It means the things you do for one another that matter. I love my baby more than he can ever know. Can't believe how lucky I am to virtually find my other half. You are my everything and couldn't be happier with things. Xoxo your queen ☺

-Hear Ye, Hear Ye, Thee Digitally Discloses
Thee's Yet Again Wandering Gaze..

"Get it Girl! Woot Woot! Ugh ..sooo jealous of how pretty you are! Love your dress bbiittch! Lovebunny, I wanna a hug.. When can I see your pwetty face?? ☹ I can't believe I didn't take your number down last nniigght like wtf we are secret bffs! Hey love! Loved meeting you last night, we hhhaavve to hang together promise?? K good."

-Interactions Brought To You By: Tender Gender
Closet Contenders..

Dear *Facebook friends*,
It is with deep disappointment I must make this
announcement. As of yesterday, I have decided I
will temporarily leave *Facebook* and all of you.

Recently my wife was in a verbal exchange *online* and was left with hurt feelings. As her loving husband, I must take her side on this. I'm not sure how long I will be away from the site, but time is the best healer. I will be sure to inform you all of my *re-instated account*. It's been fun *friends* and family. Until then, William B.

–Are You Sure You Want To Report Willam B. For His Improper Use Of The Site? Send. Are You Sure You Want To Report Suspicious Babyboomer Use On Facebook? Send.

Check out the twinnies Kayla and Kyle's birthday bash! Love having weekends off to see these cuddle bugs!! Wish their dad were here and not away on business for a month UGH!

-Dear Mr. Predator: Our *Photo Album* Here. Our Address Here. Our Household Demographics Digitally Disclosed Here. Our Number of Potential Dangerous Pets To Watch Out For Here...

Through famine, through migration, we still stand a proud nation. Faced dictators' head on we did. Discovered lands up and beyond we did. It is said our inner peasant still bleeds red white and blue. But these factors pale in comparison to the feeling of a removed *YouTube video review*..

–United We Stand: A Population Of Stagnation, We Do..

Reporting to you live, from your local news. Statistics say to *users* expect less *likes* and less *views*. What once was considered a youth haven, lurks the world war two offspring raven. Swooping and swarming in on the *shares*, dares, bewares and deliberate swears. Ripping out of the soil the demographic worm, changing the *platform* from party pics to perms..

-Molested & Tested Is The Invested..

Wow Mom and Dad, did you see that skunk?
That hawk? That owl? That albino chipmunk?
How were those faces carved on the cliffs? *Send
me those pics in jpegs not tiffs* ? Can you fathom
the waterfall drop? What about the poison
potency of the frog that went plop? Mom, Dad,

you think I could ever design architecture this inventive or smart? "Hang on a *second*, we were *mentioned* sweetheart.."

–Child Retention Rate Receding..

"Yikes! You still look gorgeous as ever Sue Ann! I guess nothing has changed since sophomore year of high school am I right everybody? I hope Rick still has his ROCKET of an arm! Maybe we could grab a cup of coffee sometime Sue Ann? All my best"

-Inappropriate *Site User* Oblivious To Target *Receiver's Status*, Situation, And *Responses* To Every Other *Picture Comment* Except His Own...

Oh jeez, I'm falling behind. I need to scoop up my daughter to avoid societal bind. Climb those pumpkins honey while I snap a *pic* ! Smile wide *like* your performing a trick! Phew I *posted* this pumpkin patch *album* in a nick of time. Before peers question "Does she do anything with her child *like* read books with rhyme?" I know I'm covered for at least sixty days, completing my deceit-ridden *social media* duty in Mary Poppineous ways..

–Accessory To Child Accessory..

Hey family! It's me. Your gas bill here.. Sorry to say, but today's purchase list I plan to smear. Thanks for understanding your need to give up certain things this week.. But if you'd *like* to *connect* with us on an even more detailed level, check out our *social media page* leak! Before you know it, we'll be *posting, inviting, tweeting, sharing; mentioning, liking, removing, re-sharing!* Just think, your gas company is the first in the pool, to establish mass-desired *social media* presence, and be finally considered "cool!"

–Business Rules #1-Know Your Boundaries. Know Your Products. Know Customer Retention..

GROUP BY BABYBOOMERS, FOR THE BABYBOOMERS..

Maldo Jr. High School (nka B.D. Maldo Middle School)

899 members

Alumni from Maldo Jr. **High** who..enjoy *sharing* memories. (If you are NOT alumni - don't *join* this *group* - you will be banned as soon as you *spam* us or someone realizes you are an imposter!)

Any *member* can *add others* to this *group*.

PLEASE make sure that the person actually went to Maldo Jr. High. We don't want a riot here!!-LOL

Please refrain from political, religious lectures or *postings*, and absolutely do NOT *spam* us! We are NOT here for solicitations of any kind.

If you do NOT belong to our alumni/*group*, then please speak up and tell us why you are here (some rivals have been welcomed-approval is needed first), otherwise you will soon be *deleted* & *BANNED* from our *group*.

-Our Deepest And Sincere Sympathies For Any Babyboomer Offspring Affected By This Via Their Household Members..

GROUP : "*Like* If You Love And Appreciate The Female Body"
Related *GROUP* : "Like If You Aren't A Male Chauvinistic Pig And Don't Enroll In *Online Groups* That Are Excuses To Exploit Women, Contribute To Illiterate, Repetitive, Misspelled,

Sentence Fragmented, Improper Punctuation
Doused, Hoodrat *Comments*.

–The Ten Gentle *Social Media* Addict's
Commandments Derivative..

I'm willing to bet that only a select few of my FB *friends* and family will *repost* and acknowledge this *post*.

"Everybody let's do this. (And, News Networks this one's for you!!..) We should flood *Facebook* with this... I pledge allegiance, to the flag, of the United States of America. *Type* The Rest Out if you feel you are patriotic, love this great country and support the troops. Oh, and *RE-POST* to see what other of your *facebook friends* love our country as much as myself and those others who have already acknowledged this."

–The Silent Remainder's *Suggestion* : Unless You Are A Veteran Yourself Or In Someway Can Relate To The Pain And Struggles Of War, Shut Your Bandwagon, Covering Your *Public Social Media* Patriotic Bases Ass Up.. Grab A .45 And Go Put Your Own Work In Overseas. There's No Room For Phony Talk Show Host *Like Suggestions* On A *Platform* Many Did *Find* Useful..

ABOUT
Worked At Richard Manches Roofing (retired)
Studied At School Of HardKnocks U

Past: Farthest Thing From Original High School
In a relationship with Carol Multiple Maiden
Names Hofferson

-Guideline And Code Of The *Online* Babyboomer
Nation...
#viveCAPSLOCKNATION

Retro Rodney Ferguson *changed his cover photo* to: A *picture* of his fraternity flag that hangs high in his front yard, in which Rodney was a *member* 20 years ago. You know, the flag that neighbors plot to discard for fear of further embarrassment? *Yesterday.*

–The Double Whammy Eyesore: 1st *Online*, 2nd Neighborhood…

Wow, what a great vacation to Pebble Beach! Great, great weather. No rain and 90's every day! Great beach, and golf. Allen made his first ever birdie and even beat his dad for the first time! He shot a 2 over 72 on the oldest golf course in Pebble Beach! Kathy Joe and Ann Louise had plenty of beach time/mom-daughter time. Ann Louise had her best finish in mini golf, second place! A great time and finished up on Sunday with our 30th anniversary of being married to the most wonderful person in the world. I love you Kathy Joe......Unfortunately (for the kids) next year on our 31st, it's just the 2 of us.....lol. So much more. Will *post pics* later.

–Social Media Company Investors: Recognize The Warning Signs And Know When To Dump Shares...

This math teacher Mike, had bought a bike, cruising the road on off days. Mike had ridden, through the *landscape* forbidden, of blacktop, gravel and construction delays. But Mike's new lifestyle comes with a price, comes with risk, a roll of the dice. When Mike discovered his favorite actor's first name was Burgess, he *switched tabs* and continued constructing his *event* to "Sturgis." All teacher Mike wanted was a day to be wild. A day to pierce his nipples. To act like a child. What math teacher Mike remembered made him not so happy. Of the great odds at his daughter's school, kids might read *posts* from her Crackpot Pappy!

-An Emotional, Physical, Digital Tear…
#MADHATTERSWAGGER

The Trouser Gifted Sea Merchants
Musician/Band
June 8
"Tonight is the big night! Get out to Prairie
Doggers Tap to hear your neighborhood
Merchants tackle tunes by #Pearl Jam, #Boston,
#Adele, #The Beatles, and more! 8pm-11pm.
Hope to see you there! Oh, feel free to bring
anybody you want! It'll be a funky time, we
promise!"

–The Area Resident Recipient Clicking Noises,
Of The Over *Messaged* -Spurring Ignores...

I never *post* like this but it is easier than calling everyone so here it goes. Surgery *update*.... I don't have *Internet* at the hospital believe it or not... Beverly's doing good. She has some shoulder pain from the surgery positioning and they are watching and measuring her output but she may stay one more day. Surgery was a success and a test will be done next week to make sure they got all the nerves. Doctor feels good about it.

-MAYDAY! MAYDAY! IT'S
BOOMERS…THEY'RE..
THEY'RE..EVERYWHERE! #CAPSLOCK
NATION

But Mr.Employer, you must understand, that that isn't me with a fifth of alcohol in my hand. "Are you sure there sonny, he looks *like* you. The gut, the Mohawk, the tacky barbwire tattoo?" Just look at the *account name*, that guy in the *picture's* name is Smoshef! How can you say that when you know my name is Joseph?

–Annual Staff *Report* : Lacks Creativity, Innovativeness, Outside Work *Activities* Pose A Threat To Company Reputation…

Barb And Timothy Daniels *liked* the city they live in *facebook page*.

–Dear Legislators: Ban, Illegalize, Fine, Penalize Up To 10 -15 Years In Prison Any And All Joint Couple *Profiles*, Banter And The *Like*..

A green light? A green light! Do you know what that means? They're on! She's on! He's On! Oh the *options*.. I must decide within the 1-2 second time glass, and hope *like* heck they don't *file* a restraint on my ass.

-As Soon As I *Log-in* Feelings…

Remember how he'd whip the dodge ball at me and Cootzy? Remember how he'd bend his leg over his head and tootzy? How bout the times he told us to check our drawers? When we'd rip ass during practice and have to mop the floors?

-Babyboomer Locker-Room Banter *Re-instated*
Through The Topic *Thread* : "Coach" …

If you lean *like* a chollo, and believe in *yolo*,
there's a certain way you *type*. From "Dam u
looks bonita mommi" to "Silencio Tommi,"
reading and writing correctly in dual languages
must be hype? Spell Check *likes* this. Google
Translate *likes* this.

-Pick A Tongue. Any Tongue...

Riddle me this: On a cheap piece of paper I stand, barely visible due to low ink, I look like a #PartyCity costume pimp, but make sure my oversized clothes never shrink. You knows who this be, by counting how many shout out artists named "Lil" are on the flyer list, I don't look *like* a very approachable fella yo, and no rockn'roll is my mutha f'n motto.

–Unappealing Amateur Hip Hop Party Invitation You Usually See Nailed To Your Local Electrical Pole. Where Every Participant Is Said To Be "A Lyrical Poet & Coming Up"…

I'm a terrific *program* ! I *suggest* you use me. I *cover* up, I enhance, instead of dieting you abuse me. I give you that Florida tan in the dead of winter. I'm often *used* to decorate tackily on couples 2nd day of dating anniversary.

-Photoshop You're My Everything, Happy 2 Weeks & Counting Baby…

You brew a grin to see a red number peek out, from your *twitter program's icon* thanks to you never *logging out*. You see a *favorite, mention* and splendid *retweet*. You *click* on the *notification* only to see it's Margarite??

-Fritz Esperanza from Brazil *favorited* your *tweet*.
"Ugh, court ttoommrrow.."
Hunan Alvaretz from Warsaw *retweeted* your
status on "My Gram Gram Janice makes thee
BBESST KEESH!"
Your Residence Remains The United States…
#fakeaccountamount

As I walk into #BuffaloWildWings, to see the pay-per-view fight, who do I see, but a table full of insight. Putting their hands up to their faces like they're blocking punches, to extending their jabs that wouldn't bring nose crunches. Could authentic boxing analysts really have come to my town? Would analysts wear in *public* stained sweatpants-like gowns? Since when are analysts not polished and clean-cut? Sporting long ponytails, three chins and a backcountry gut?

-Bandwagon Connoisseurs..
#THE BIG GAME AD CAMPAIGN TARGET
MARKET

Toby the hermit, as lanky as Kermit, in high school never went out. On Friday nights, Toby would reach new heights, snagging a slushee and X-Box his heart out. But once Toby hit college, he put down his Code Red Mountain Dew, put down his controller, and embraced a brew. First day having a domestic sort, The second *posting* a *pic* of a micro-brewed sized quart.

-Seasoned Beer Connoisseur; 19 Years Of Age. Don't Believe Him? Just *View* The Craft Bottle He *Posted* ! I Mean, Right!…

Riddle Me This: I stand behind skyscrapers, holding one of #Starbuck's seasonal latte creations. Rocking a socialite Pea coat with legit indentations. I pose for *pictures* at unusual spots, sporting a nose-ring like #Tupac, I point my finger *like* I let out shots. The leggings I wear are #AmeliaBedelia style, wearing #Ponch's aviators as I refuse to smile. My *favorite* thing to tell peeps is "I don't *like* to vote." Every *other pic* in my *album* is a #MarilynMonroe quote. I am?

-That "Spill Your Guts Out *Online* " Kind Of Hipster. The City! The City Is *Where* It's At. That's Sssoo *Like* The City!

I think I'll check my *facebook*, hell might as well I'm on the john. Let me take out my phone and quickly *log-on*. Would you look at that! All the Birthday wishes.. All The "Another Year's Here" and "Best Wishes!" But between real tight, and squeezed solid in there, is the "happy bday" wish, that was *typed* without care..

-Lack Luster Bday Wishes *via facebook*. Happy bday This Pal..

Katie D. listened to #OneDirection on #Spotify 2min ago.
Katie D. listened to #JustinTimberlake on #Spotify 1min ago.
Katie D. listened to #Hanson on #Spotify 2min ago.

Katie D. #instagramed a selfie duck lips via android 1min ago.
Katie D. #liked the characters on a kid's network, who in real life, are in their late 20's, but the network does their best to make them look tweeny.

-Send Prescription For Your *Newsfeed's* Aches..

How come I can't *find* you? I *typed* in your name..
I *searched* you for 10 minutes. All I got was
Corey Haim. Is it because I didn't call? *Message*
or *Invite* you Cin? Was it because of this
weekend's *album* that I didn't *tag* you in?

-Temporarily *blocking* person for 2 weeks.
Social Media Time-Out...

"Honey are you sure you turned everything in?
Your paperwork? Your birth certificate? Your
Social Security Pin?" Yes dear relax, those things

wont help me win. It's that *public figure page* on *facebook*, starring me, your next Alderman.

- # Of *Likes* For Campaigning Alderman's *Public Figure Page* : 7. #supportiveneighborsonhisstreet

Fran Fromier changed her background picture to "It's 5 o'Clock Somewhere."

Fran Fromier listed she is mother of *Nathan Fromier* and *Becky Fromier*.

Besides *working* as Nurse, *Fran Fromier* listed works at *"MOM"*

-Spare Us This Day, Our Daily *Newsfeeds*...

In a land of "durs" and phony "forsures", lurks the *photograph* caper. Letting his hanging tongue linger, while raising a middle finger, Ladies and gentlemen: The #TupacShakur shape-shifter.

-Dear Mama, Just Me Against The *Social Media* World…

Bulletin : I NEED Numbers *like*..NOW
pwease?!?!? Lost my phone AGGAIIN UGH…
Help Help! K? Good. Xoxo Stephy!!

News Bulletin : By Submitting Your Numbers For
The 3rd Time, You Are Now Enabling This

Careless & Rather Child-*Like* Behavior. But Do Know, You WILL Get The Chance To Witness *Bulletin* Again. Should You, The Male, Feel You Have A Chance With This Lady..

Riddle me this: I'm sitting in my computer chair in my room. Mouth full of gold and silver teeth with lettering encrusted "Vrroom." The "Vrroom" symbolizes my *interests* in fast, luxurious cars. I'm holding some twenties, tens, ones, and more than likely to soon end up behind bars.
I am?

-Small Time Marijuana Peddling, Middle Class, High School Kid, Who Removes Costume *Like* Clothing When Parents Pull In Driveway In Their Acura And Lexus. Only To Tell Them How Wonderful Lacrosse Practice Was...

As I punch the clock, I gather my things. My shovels, my rakes, my blue-collar things. The morning sucked with all the bugs.. All the gnats. All The Grubs.. It's not lunch yet, but hell, I'll stop

in. At Ristorante De Subs, why oh why did I
check-in ?

-Dale, After Work Can You Stop In My Office? #OVERTHERADIOANDTHROUGHTHEWOODS TOREPRIMANDINGYOUGO

Soccer players be *like*..Basketball players be *like*..Animals be *like*..Hobos be *like*..Gargoyles be *like*.. Pokemon be *like*…Munchkins be *like*..Tall Tale Characters be *like*..Lambchop The Puppet be *like*..Cold nipples be *like*..

-Users Be Like.. "S.O.S."

Sheem sheem shala beam. Reem reem lickity leem. Abra cadabra, a la whip cream. See. *Share*. Poof! IT'S A *MEME* !

-Poof! Goes my *desktop* sleeping…Poof! Goes my *feed's* weeping. Poof! Goes my *settings* from *active* to *de-active*. Poof! Goes my membership - *joining* another *platform* more attractive..

You cannot have a free society unless you have a free enterprise system. And you cannot have a free enterprise system unless you have a Constitution that limits the power of government. Our civil liberties give us the freedom to affect our own futures and to *use* the opportunities that a free enterprise system gives us to prosper as we would wish. Because of this, people have flocked to this country for generations now. They have escaped tyrannical governments that limited liberty and as a result economic and social freedoms that we have enjoyed here in the U.S. All of that is changing. Our people don't believe in free enterprise and a controlled government that stays out of the affairs of its people. We don't believe in civil liberties or we take them for granted. Our Bill of Rights is under constant attack by a government that does not want to be strangled by the Constitution either. Our people no longer look for the freedom to be able to affect their own prosperity. They look to unrestrained big government to give them everything they want. Lenin and communism came into power by promising the masses that government was the answer to their struggles.....the same promise our government is making *today*..

-In Response To Nephew's Deliberate *Post* To Fluster His Uncle: "Who CAAARREES About Politics And Gov't UGH, FML.."
#SillyBoomer; *Social Media's* For Kids!

How could we have done it? Done it without you?
Without your support, who knows what we'd do!
Your encouragement and actions, topple the
apparatus. When you showed us support by
liking our updated chemotherapy *status*..

-Scapegoat Of The Lost Human Touch...

Look at those empties! Look at that mess! Look
at Maggie's hideous dress! Did that pricey lamp

shatter because of those two..? Shirtless buffoons wrestling *like* their *home* is the zoo?

-Let The Big Bad Wolf In 3 Little Piggies To Your Party; But Never A Five Years Out High School Wrestler…

I can't believe he'd give her up *like* that…Is it just me? Or does anyone feel the main character should haven't have tried to save his own ass and take the wrap for his lover?.. Now she's doing 10 YEARS thanks to main character. Lliikke how is that the ending to the season?..

-Spoiler Spoils, Blooms The *NewsFeed* Bad
Seed...

I've had enough. I can't bear it anymore. If I see one more #teehee, I'll puke on the floors. It's time to *de-activate* my *account* and finally attack my chores. I quote the Amish Raven: Never more, never more.

-Finishing Your Chores, You End Up Creating A Phony *Account* Using Your Middle Name First, Then Mother's Maiden Name Last; So You Can Still Snoop, Creep And Gossip. But, "You Don't Do That *Posting, Tweeting* Junk Anymore.." #right

Isn't that?.. Yeah! It totally is! See the sweater? See the flower patterns? See the hair-like frizz? Oh those are the boots from the #BradyBunch Movie! Isn't that the chest hair of #MagnumP.I.? How Groovy! I can't believe he didn't have that mop up in a ponytail or bun? Correct me if I'm wrong, but doesn't Dad look like an extra from #SanfordAndSon?

-Mo-Town Swagger, Vinyl Record Bagger, "I've Got A Golden Ticket!" Bragger... #WonkaKid

Seriously? Wipe your nose Damien. How the hell does a third grader not pack his lunch?? Omg HHEELLP. Uggh.. These brats need to be quiet!

Trying to work on that Master's Degree homework WOOT WOOT! #movinonup

-Recent Elementary Teacher, School District Ordered "Fire Of The Month" *Feature*, A *Social* - Remorseful Creature..

Sherry Marie Vaughn Atkins: Head-Master Phillip Woodzner wouldn't tolerate the boys not wearing belts. If you didn't have one on, you were sent home to get one. Can't imagine what he would do if he caught anyone smoking cigarettes. You could hear a pin drop in the halls during class. A lot different than today. But it taught all of us respect.

-1st *Comment Via* The 30 Year High-School Re-Union Boomer Orchestrated *Event*.

Wait,...Multiple Boomers *Via* The Same Room?... #ThatShitCrayola

Yet again, I sit alone. Yet again, resort to my phone. Morning in, morning out. I can't escape blue-collar tout. I don't have a *favorite* team. I don't have a sports logo on my coat seam. If I bring up movie lines from #LemonySnicket, co-workers glare and even so does the cricket. Blue-collar minds are all wired the same. What's broken? Who done it? Did ya catch "the big game?" Little do they know, I give a flying fuck. I prefer quality television, like a dynasty full of ducks.

-Repost If Your *Work Place* Lunch-Table Matches *Description*. You Are Not Alone. #TickTockPunchClock

Some say Shalom. Some say Hola. Some say Hello and some say Aloha. Some say Xie Xie. While others say Dank. Some say Spasibo; all ways to thank. It is with these thanks that come with *retweets* ; *favorites, re-pins, now following* sweets. These treats that meet the *blogger* expectation, create a more connected nation.

-Tyrant Leader Rant Portal = *Social Media...*

A cat high-fiving a bat! A rat swinging a baseball-bat! A chipmunk wearing earmuffs! A platypus in handcuffs! A raccoon steering a sailboat! A corrupt politician in a crocodile infested moat! A family of rabbits wearing #ChicagoBears jerseys! Autographed pic of #DeathWish character Paul Kersey!

-Babyboomer *Post-Work Meme Shares…*

A *picture* was once *shared* consisting of #Batman in a bathtub. That *picture* was called "BATHMAN." It was that *picture* that *received* ten likes. And *comments* in the ballpark of "na na na na na na BATMANNN!!"

-Boomer breaks down the Berlin Wall of *Social Media* : #Photoshop…

Kelly Joe Ritter O'Shay *shared* "Mom's Secret Danish Recipe" 2min ago. Kelly multiple maiden names O'Shay did in fact *list* the actual recipe. But to spare you, the reader, any further embarrassment or heartache, these *comments* came *following* Kelly Joe Ritter O'Shay's recipe *posting* :

-Stew Windbocker are u trying to break my diet Kelly??

Alice (Yards) Lane don't worry I won't tell your mom of your devious ways he he he he

Linda Scott (Realty) I think I might try that for my boys.. Although Josh does have a severe peanut allergy. So maybe I won't include the pecans… William on the other hand, WILL EAT ANYTHING! Lol…

DON'T DATE MY DAUGHTER MEME. I LOVE MY KIDS MEME. ANIMALS CAPTURED ON CAMERA DOING HUMAN THINGS MEME. SPORTS RIVALRY MEME. FAMILYS ARE SWEET BUT HAVE THEIR NUTS MEMES. WHAT A GIRL WANTS MEMES. WHAT MEN LIKE MEMES. HATE DISEASES MEMES. PATRIOTIC MEMES. POLITICAL MEMES. MISSING LOVED ONE MEMES. WHAT I LEARNED IN SCHOOL MEMES. IT IS WITH THESE MEMES THAT WE COMMUNICATE. HOW WE INTERACT, HOW WE RELATE. IF WASN'T FOR MEMES, ALL WOULD BE TRUE; THE RUMORS. A MEME-LESS VIRTUAL

SOCIETY WOULD BE THE DOWNFALL OF
THE BABYBOOMERS.

-The Unspoken Rule Of *Posting* One *Meme*
Monthly... #SPEAKEASY GREAT PEOPLE OF
THE #CAPSLOCKNATION

Bertha May Bunions *shared* "How Many *Likes* For This *Pic* ??!"

Five years ago, an injured and ill raccoon called "Robber" was found in the street after a fight with dogs. Robber was nursed back to health by this man's patience, love and determination...How many *Likes* deserve this man?!!!! (*Picture* consists of middle age man coddling a raccoon who seems to be pissed off that a human is holding him hostage.)

-BOOMERS: #TheAndyGriffithShow, Despite
What's Been Said, Was In Fact A SHOW.
Raccoon Classification=Wild. #Opie *likes* this.
sent via 1960's…
#RABID IS THE BEHOLDER

Every now and then, you'll see a *post*. Of inspiration, from an unlikely *host*. "Reinvention isn't something man discovers, it's something he creates." Mucho gracias college #barfly, what's next? A quote from #BillGates?

-Host's *Friends* (Who Believe Fraternity Movies Are Real Life) like this. #Era De Motivational Quotes De Un-Practicing Sources...

"We have better rates!" We have better gyms!
"We have better systems, blasting better hymns!"
Real athletes pump heavy iron! "Real athletes
complete obstacles!" We have members with true
strength! "Your outdoor business sign light dims!"

-Crossfitters Vs Weightlifters. When will the #DigitalGangRivalry stop..

Come on already! How couldn't anyone see?
See my new motto. Created specifically by me?
This is wrong. This is unjust. To rush to my log-in
& change my twitter tag line is a MUST!

-Social Media Addict @tweetaholic

Looking forward to the memories of right now..
Today

-Social Media Addict@tweetaholic
Making mistakes. One day at a time..
1 Day Ago

-Social Media Addict@tweetaholic
I'm 23 years old. I love pizza, money and all
other general things most people enjoy. Staying
un-original and parroting when I can..
2 Days Ago

Congratulations! You won the bid. One week till
arrival. Keep cool and under lid. Ding Dong it's
here! Far-out man, delivery was on point! It's time

to claim my most precious prize: the remainder of
a #Simon&Garfunkel joint!

-2nd Pic Of Profile Picture Album Of Then Hippie,
To Now Board Member Of Fortune 500
Company.. #flowerpowerresistance

If you think you know where the button is. Where to refresh your page. Where to update info on your biz. Don't be so sure the environment will remain the same. We must compete with our rivals, in this constant changing of layout game.

-Whereabouts Pouts, Other Platforms User Scouts…

#LOL Happy Addicts Sing Along: You, only you, wear your posting suit. Wear your posting suit, wear your posting suit. You, only you, wear your posting suit, the suit you've sewn bearing perhaps poisonous blogging fruit.

-Pursue Common Sense Thread Of Your Own
Suit; Pursue Not The Company's Suit With Suit.
#USER BRUISER CANNONBALLS SINK
DIGITAL & REAL-LIFE SHIPS; NOT LOOSE
SETTINGS.

.

Catch me if you can #App maker! Catch me if you can #Ebook market shaker! My name's NICHE and these are examples in which I relate, like the United State's Copyright Office's rule: first to register, the only to create.

-2010's Digital Goldrush.. #My Mine Is Your #Mine See?

Explaining opening a *new tab*, to seeing your parents multiple *accounts*, to forgotten *passwords*, to iTunes credit amounts. Your parents are still *users*, while occasional *platform* bruisers, contributing squat to daily *trends*, but more in the vicinity of "Remember that seen from Hoosiers?"

-Failed Attempts = Credited Attempts On The Road To *Social Media* Proficiency...

#BOOMER SIGHTING!

Retweet! Post! Share! Re-Pin!

#BOOMER SIGHTING!

Retweet! Post! Share! Re-Pin!

#BOOMER SIGHTING!

Retweet! Post! Share! Re-Pin!

#BOOMER SIGHTING!

Retweet! Post! Share! Re-Pin!